W9-CHQ-673

Adventures in ODYSSEY.

WELCOME TO ODYSSEY

THE START OF
SOMETHING
BIG

Don't miss a single adventure! Listen regularly to *Adventures in Odyssey* on the radio! Check your local listings or contact us directly for a complete programming schedule for your area.

Call 1-800-A-FAMILY or write:

Focus on the Family

Colorado Springs, CO 80995

Or visit us on the web at www.family.org

Published in Nashville, Tennessee, by Tommy Nelson™, a division of Thomas Nelson, Inc.

Library of Congress Cataloging-in-Publication Data
Lollar, Phil.
    Welcome to Odyssey : the start of something big! / by Phil Lollar; art by DRi Artworks.
        p. cm.
    Summary: Dylan is bored when he moves with his family to the small town of Odyssey, until God answers his parents' prayers and helps Dylan find some new friends.
    ISBN 1-56179-104-0
    [1. Helpfulness Fiction. 2. Christian life Fiction.] I. DRi Artworks.
II. Title.
PZ7.L8312We 1999
[E]—dc21
                                                            99-42762
                                                                CIP

Printed in the United States of America.

99 00 01 02 PCC 9 8 7 6 5 4 3 2

WELCOME TO ODYSSEY

THE START OF SOMETHING BIG

Written by
PHIL LOLLAR

Illustrated by **DRi Artworks**

Thomas Nelson, Inc.
Nashville

"My life is over."

Dylan Taylor plopped down on his front steps. *It's bad enough being the new kid in town*, he thought, fingering his baseball. *But in a town as small as Odyssey, it's the worst.* He was used to the big city—amusement parks, major league baseball, and a skatepark with two vert ramps. In Odyssey, the skatepark also doubled as the sidewalk. Dylan sighed.

"I'll never like it here!"

He heard a noise above him, then he looked up and saw
a strange sight. A hot air balloon attached to a large boat
with propellers hovered for a moment, then it sped away.

Dylan tried to get a better view. Suddenly a brown-and-tan streak raced into his yard, knocked him down, and sat on his chest. The streak was a dog, and the tag around his neck read, "Sherman Prop. J.A.W."

"Get off me, you mutt!" Dylan yelled, and he was
answered with a slurpy kiss. "Ugh! I said get off!"
Dylan pushed Sherman away. The dog barked happily
then grabbed the baseball in his mouth and took off.
"Come back here!" Dylan hollered.

They raced down the street, through the next block,
and into a park. Dylan was so intent on catching Sherman
that he wasn't watching where he was going.

He plowed right into a girl carrying a huge box. She went flying and so did the box, spilling its contents all over the grass.

"Nice one," said the girl. Dylan helped her to her feet.

"I'm sorry! That dog stole my ball!"

"What dog?"

Dylan looked around. Sherman was gone.

The girl started refilling the box. Dylan helped and was surprised to see that it contained party favors—hats, noisemakers, and streamers.

"They're for where I work," the girl said. "And I could really use a hand carrying the box. Please?"

Dylan really wanted to find Sherman. But the girl did ask nicely, and he *had* knocked her down, after all. "Okay," he said. The girl smiled. "Great! By the way, I'm Connie." Dylan introduced himself. "I'm Dylan."

And while he was speaking, the strange machine again streaked across the sky and then disappeared from view.

They carried the box to a huge, Victorian mansion in
the middle of the park. "You work here?" asked Dylan.
Connie nodded. "It's a combination ice cream parlor and
discovery emporium called 'Whit's End.'"

"Cool," said Dylan. But the place was even cooler on the inside. It was bright and colorful and filled with stairwells, passages, and hallways that all looked like they could lead to an adventure.

Just then, Dylan heard Sherman barking outside. Dylan raced toward the door and barreled into a skinny young man with glasses, knocking him over. "Just the person I wanted to see," he said as he got up. "I'm Eugene Meltsner, resident genius." At the door, Connie rolled her eyes. "Got those balloons blown up yet, Mr. Resident Genius?" Eugene smiled sheepishly. "I was hoping our young friend here might assist me with that task."

Dylan reluctantly agreed to help Eugene and followed him outside to a large contraption. "It's a little invention of mine called a heliometer," he explained. "It automatically inflates balloons with helium. However, it has a problem shutting off when the balloon is full. That's where you come in." Eugene showed Dylan how to work the shut-off valve, and they quickly inflated most of the balloons.

They were filling the last one when Sherman suddenly ran up and knocked Dylan down again. He jumped up and was just about to retrieve his ball when he heard Eugene yell, "Assistance! Dylan—the shut-off valve!" Somehow, the hose of the heliometer had gotten inside Eugene's shirt, inflating it and lifting him off the ground!

Dylan quickly grabbed the valve, closing it. Eugene slowly sank back to earth. But behind him, in the sky, Dylan again saw the strange machine fly over.

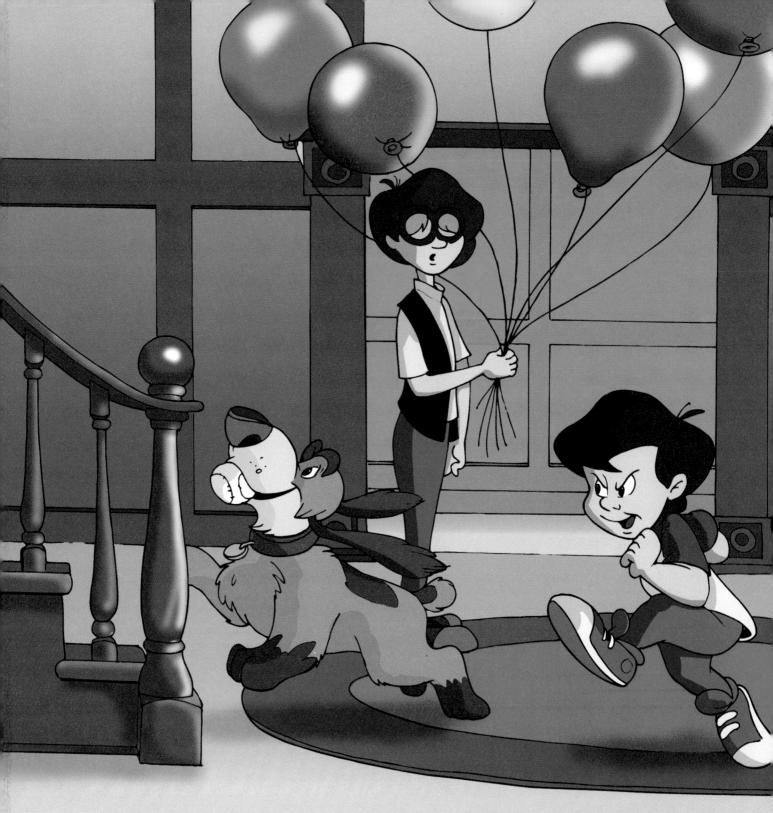

They had just taken the balloons inside when Sherman reappeared and ran upstairs. "I'll get you this time, you crazy mutt!" yelled Dylan. Sherman bounded up and down the steps and raced through the hallways and passages, with Dylan following closely behind.

Finally, Dylan cornered Sherman in a large atrium. "Alright," he said breathlessly, "drop the ball." The dog obeyed, and Dylan snatched it up.

"Congratulations!" said a voice behind him. Dylan wheeled around. In the center of the atrium was an older man with a big mustache. He was standing right next to the strange flying machine! Sherman ran to the man and stood beside him. The man smiled. "I'm glad you're here! I'm John Avery Whittaker. But most folks call me Whit."

"Wait a minute," said Dylan. "John Avery Whittaker—
J.A.W.—like on Sherman's tag!"
Whit nodded. "He's my dog, though sometimes he
doesn't act like it."

"And this is your machine?"

"Uh-huh—the Strata-Flyer. It gets me around town," Whit answered.

"Could I have a ride?"

"Maybe later." Whit said. He reached into the Strata-Flyer and pulled out a large, folded cloth. "First, I really need your help putting up this banner in the other room."

Dylan growled with frustration. "Help, help, help! That's all I've been doing all day! Can't anyone do anything for themselves around here?"

Whit frowned. "Never mind, then. Come on, Sherman."

They turned to leave, and Dylan suddenly felt very bad. "Wait!" Whit and Sherman stopped and faced him. Dylan walked up to them. "Okay. I'll help you." Whit smiled, and they walked together into the main room. "I'm sorry, Mr. Whittaker. It's just that the Strata-Flyer is the most exciting thing I've seen in this town."

"Does that mean you're bored living in Odyssey?"

"Of course! There's nothing to do!"

"Have you been bored today?"

Dylan thought for a moment, then realized that he hadn't been bored—not at all. "No," he said. "In fact, this day has been pretty packed."

"And all without a ride on the Strata-Flyer. Imagine that." Whit smiled again. "See, Dylan, the best way to stop being bored is to help others. It's called 'loving your neighbor as yourself.'"

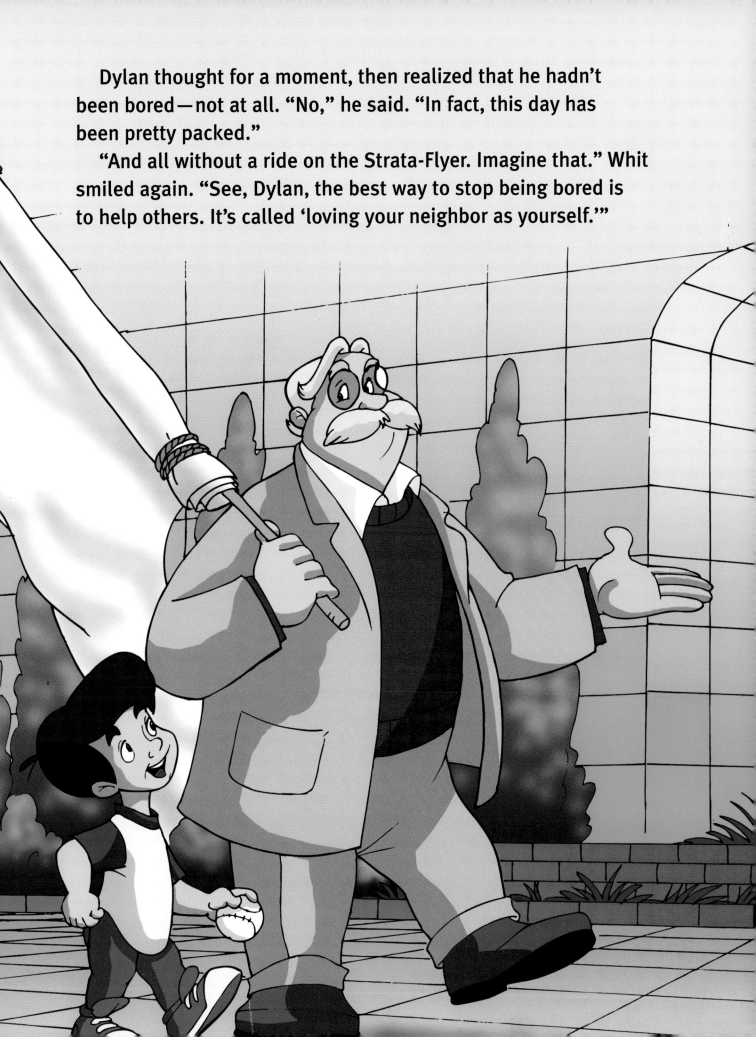

Dylan remembered that verse—Matthew 22:39.
His parents had taught him that when he was barely old
enough to understand it. And suddenly, he was glad Whit
reminded him of it.

"Okay," said Whit. "I've got the ropes attached to the
banner. You take that side, I'll take this side, and on three,
we'll open it. Ready? One . . . two . . . three!"

Suddenly everyone—including Dylan's parents and little sister Jessie—rushed in and yelled, "Surprise!" Dylan realized the party he had helped set up was for him! He turned to his mom and asked, "But . . . how?"

"Your dad and I saw how unhappy you were," Mom explained. "So we called Mr. Whittaker, and he came up with this idea."

"We've been praying for new, good friends for you," added Dad. "I'd say God has answered that prayer, wouldn't you?"

"Absolutely!" exclaimed Dylan. "Thanks, Mom and Dad. And you, too, Mr. Whittaker."

Whit smiled. "Don't mention it. Now, how about that ride in the Strata-Flyer?"

As they took to the air, Dylan thought, *I guess my life isn't over after all. In fact, I think it's just beginning!*